Tomahawk Beckwourth

My Life and Adventures

Adapted by Michael Cox

Illustrated by Barbara Lofthouse

PACIFIC
LEARNING

© 2004 **Pacific Learning**
© 2003 Adapted by **Michael Cox**
Illustrated by **Barbara Lofthouse c/o Artist Partners**
Photography: Cover photo by C. Waldo Love/Colorado Historical Society; p. 1 Eastman Studio Portrait/Plumas County Museum; pp. 4–5 Corel; p. 5 Geoffrey Clements/Corbis UK Ltd.; p. 7 Hulton/Archive/Getty Images; pp. 16–17 Geoffrey Clements/Corbis UK Ltd.; pp. 18–19 Hulton/Archive/Getty Images; p. 23 Corbis UK Ltd.; pp. 24–25 Joseph Sohm; Visions of America/Corbis UK Ltd.; p. 43 Missouri Historical Society, St. Louis; p. 51 Mary Evans Picture Library; p. 55 Bridgeman Art Library; p. 60 Bettmann/Corbis UK Ltd.; p. 61 Bettmann/Corbis UK Ltd.; p. 78 Hulton/Archive/Getty Images; pp. 78–79 Corel
U.S. edit by **Alison Auch**

All rights reserved. No part of this publication may be reproduced or transmitted in any form or by any means, electronic or mechanical, including photocopying, recording, taping, or any information storage and retrieval system, without permission in writing from the publisher.

This Americanized Edition of *Tomahawk Beckwourth,* originally published in England in 2003, is published by arrangement with Oxford University Press.

08 07
10 9 8 7 6 5 4 3 2

Published by
    Pacific Learning
    P.O. Box 2723
    Huntington Beach, CA 92647-0723
    www.pacificlearning.com

ISBN: 978-1-59055-446-3
PL-7613

Printed in U.S.A

Contents

		Page
Introduction		4
Chapter 1	The Howling Wilderness	6
Chapter 2	Mountain Man Beckwourth	15
Chapter 3	Bull's Robe Beckwourth	32
Chapter 4	Swamp Warfare	43
Chapter 5	Santa Fe to California	51
Chapter 6	My Beautiful Valley	62
Chapter 7	My Betrayal of Friends	70
Story Background		78
Index		80
Glossary		80

Introduction

When Christopher Columbus landed in the Americas in 1492, people were already living there. These people, now known as Native Americans, had been there for at *least* 15,000 years. Christopher Columbus called them Indians because he mistakenly thought America was an island in the East Indies.

Soon after Columbus's landing, Europeans rushed to America to claim great chunks of it for themselves. The country was vast and home to many Native American tribes. It was teeming with wildlife, including grizzly bears, deer, mountain lions, and a hundred million buffalo.

By 1800, after the United States gained independence from Great Britain, the country's East Coast was settled. Europeans were displacing the Native Americans and began importing Africans to work as slaves.

The area that was known as the "Wild West" was explored by many of its new inhabitants. One of them was James (Jim)

Beckwourth, the son of a white landowner and an African-American slave. Born around 1800, he lived an incredible life, trapping, blazing trails, living among Native Americans, and leading wagon trains.

Tragically, by 1890 most Native Americans had been killed or driven from their homes. Of the millions of buffalo, only 541 remained.

Jim Beckwourth was a great frontiersman, who explored the landscape and lived among its people as the country changed forever.

A painting of the American wilderness

CHAPTER

The Howling Wilderness

I think it must have been around the time I had the fight with Mad Bill Payne that some young fellow asked me to tell him the scariest thing that had ever happened to me. I couldn't. Why? Because I've had so many terrifying and hair-raising things happen to me, I've lost count!

Truth is, ever since I was knee-high to a grasshopper, I've spent my whole life dodging death and danger. Yet it occurs to me now, that a bullet, arrow, or wild critter is going to get me sooner or later. So, in these pages, I'm going to write down some of my adventures and scrapes. I won't include all of them, though, because that would mean a book a hundred times bigger than this one!

CHAPTER 1

My name's James "Tomahawk" Beckwourth, and, during the last sixty years or so, I've lived and fought my way through some of the wildest and most thrilling times in America's history. I've battled with Indians, Mexicans, white men, and black men.

I've almost starved to death, frozen to death, and near been killed to death with tomahawks and guns. I've blazed trails in the Rocky Mountains, lived as an Indian chief, been a fur trapper, saloon keeper, trader, **express rider**, farmer, horse thief, and army scout. Seems I've done it all!

I've led wagon trains halfway across America and discovered a route through the mountains to California – the Beckwourth Pass, named after me. It's hard to believe I'm still here to tell the tale.

First off, I'll describe myself, so you've got some sort of picture of me that you can carry in your head.

I'm what many folk describe as a hardscrabble sort of man.

I dress in fringed buckskin shirts, leggings, and moccasins, and I stand more than six and a half feet tall. My black hair is long, and at one time it reached down past my waist. My skin's black too, but not as black as my hair, and over the years it's been scarred by bullets, arrows, and war axes.

My ears are pierced, and I wear gold earrings and chains and braid my hair or tie it with ribbons. I'm strong and burly, and I'm a pleasant man who enjoys singing and having a good, hearty laugh.

As to my skills, they're many: I speak English, French, and Spanish – and Indian languages too. I know the Indian ways better than anyone and can track, hunt, and scout. I'm an expert with a dagger, tomahawk, and gun, and I'm a skillful horseman who knows all kinds of amazing tricks. I can ride a galloping horse bareback, then hang upside down so my hair brushes the ground.

Now I'll tell you a little bit about my folks. My pa was Sir Jennings Beckwith, whose family came from England to America generations ago. He was an educated man with noble ancestors going back to the days of the **Norman Conquest**. My own great-granddaddy (times about fifty, I reckon!) helped William whip Harold at the Battle of Hastings in 1066 and was rewarded with a title and lands. This explains why my own pa was a "sir"... May he rest in peace.

My ma wasn't nearly as highfalutin' as my pa. She was a black slave whose family had been brought to America from Africa to work on the **plantations**. I don't exactly know how my ma and pa met, but they did, and then along I came.

I was born around 1800 in Frederick County, Virginia, which is where I lived with my folks and my twelve brothers and sisters.

Some time later, we moved to a backwoods settlement near St. Louis, Missouri. It was a howling wilderness of a place surrounded by huge forests, home to Indians and grizzly bears and all manner of other perilous things. While my pa and the settlers worked the land, they'd divide themselves into two

CHAPTER 1

groups. One would work, and one would guard against Indian attacks. They also built a log blockhouse in the center of our little settlement. At the first sign of danger, we'd all hustle in there and defend our lives.

Growing up there, we kids soon learned the ways of the woods and how to watch out for ourselves. I'll never forget the day when I was nine and Pa sent me off to get a sack of flour from a mill a few miles away.

On the way back, I went to see my friends who lived close by. As I rode my horse up to their backyard fence, I saw something that made my blood run cold and tears fill my eyes. Stretched out on the grass before me were the bodies of my little pals and their ma and pa. They'd all been killed by marauding Indians! What made me really shake from head to toe was when I saw that they had all been scalped.

So this is how I grew up. During my childhood, my pa taught me how to behave like a gentleman and to read and write and do numbers. When I got a little bit older and was getting strong, I went to work for a blacksmith in St. Louis. He and I didn't see eye to eye, though. Then, when I started seeing a very commendable young lady, we had a proper falling out. I was late for work one morning, and he yelled at me. So I yelled back. Before I knew it, we were trading blows. I soon got the better of him and had him on his knees. Then the sheriff arrived, so I had to skedaddle, fast as greased lightning.

CHAPTER 1

There was no going back after that, and soon after, I sneaked aboard a boat that was bound for Fever River. I'd heard that was where men were mining for lead and there was money to be made.

Fever River was a rough-and-tumble place. Folks lived in huts and tents, perched precariously on muddy riverbanks. Life was full of strife. There was typhoid and scurvy everywhere, and the settlers spent long, miserable winters hunkered down in the mine shafts for warmth and safety.

There were Indians at Fever River too. They sometimes gave trouble to the miners and settlers, but they didn't bother me. Often, I was out wandering in the woods when I'd come across a band of them cutting up a deer they'd killed, and I'd join them. They soon became my friends and divulged to me the choicest places for hunting.

After spending about eighteen months at Fever River, I decided to roam farther and caught a steamboat to New Orleans in Louisiana. But then, unexpectedly, I caught something else. I caught the yellow fever. Unfortunately, this forced me to return to my father's house. I wasn't there long, though! I was now hankering to be off again, looking for adventure and fame.

CHAPTER

Mountain Man Beckwourth

In the summer of 1824, after my recovery from yellow fever, I heard General William H. Ashley was taking a trapping expedition out west. Suddenly, I wanted more than anything to see the Rocky Mountains and the great western wilderness I'd heard so much about. I signed up in a flash!

Now, before I go further with my tale, I must tell you that just before I was born, all of the land that lay between the Mississippi River and the Rockies was claimed by the French. Then, in 1803, **Napoleon Bonaparte** sold it to the United States, more than doubling the size of our country. The thing was, no one knew the first thing about our 800,000 square miles of new territory!

There were no real maps, no roads or trails. So, back in the 1820s, when I was young and eager for excitement, all of the American West was still a mysterious place. It was literally covered by mountains, forests, and thousands of miles of grassy plains. This was Indian land.

CHAPTER 2

It was chock-full of eagles, bears, mountain lions, elk, buffalo, deer, and beavers. In other words, it was an adventurer's paradise! What more could a thrill-seeking fellow ask for?

The American West

Moving west around 1865

All kinds of brave and daring people were forging their way into the Wild West, seeking fame and fortune. Many drowned in rivers, got lost, starved, froze, or perished at the hands of the Indians and the claws of grizzlies and mountain lions. Others, like Jim Bridger, Kit Carson, Jedediah Smith, and I made our names by blazing new trails. We paved the way for the settlers who later followed us in the thousands, building shantytowns that would soon turn into the amazingly dynamic, exciting cities of America.

So, in 1824, bursting with excitement, I set off on my first trapping expedition with General Ashley's outfit, the Rocky Mountain Fur Company. I planned to make my fortune from furs while gaining fame from the way I handled the tough times I encountered. Let me tell you, things did get awfully tough!

We set off, a party of thirty trappers and hunters. We had fifty packhorses, carrying what we were certain was enough food and supplies to get us through the winter. How wrong we were.

Our food was gone in no time. Then the weather turned against us. I'd never known it was possible to be so cold, tired, miserable, and hungry. Soon, I was thinking I'd rather be back with that loathsome blacksmith than trudging through the waist-high snowdrifts and howling blizzards that turned us all into living snowmen. Things got so bad that we were forced to kill and eat some of our horses. After that, we had to become pack animals ourselves.

General Ashley gave orders for the best shots in our party to search for game, so I set

CHAPTER 2

off with my rifle. After a short time, I spied a duck, which I then killed. I'm ashamed to say that I ate that duck, giving no thought to my starving friends back at camp.

I felt bad about my behavior, vowing that from that moment on, I would share my last cracker, my last penny, or my only blanket with a friend in need. Fortunately, I was able to do just that. A mere few minutes after my appalling act of selfishness, I spied a large elk buck and brought it down with one shot.

Then, as I dragged it back to camp, a huge, snarling wolf came bounding toward me! This I also brought down with a bullet in its brain. Some time later, I also bagged three more good-sized elk. I finally returned to our camp laden with meat and was greeted as a hero.

However, the cold doubles men's hunger, and it wasn't long before our meat was gone. We were ravenous. Blizzards turned our flesh blue and our blood to slush, and just when we feared we couldn't last another night, six Indians walked into our camp. With much hand waving, they showed us they wanted us to follow them.

They seemed friendly enough, so we did. Soon, we arrived at their tepees, where they showed us enormous kindness, feeding us and looking after our horses for many weeks to come. So, as a result of this generous act, we survived the winter.

When spring arrived, we left our Indian friends and began trapping once more.

We now fell in love with the land we had hated throughout the winter. I hardly know

CHAPTER 2

A tepee in winter. A Native American woman is carrying a bundle of sticks into her home. When a fire is lit inside, these tentlike constructions can be extraordinarily warm.

how to describe the magical beauty of spring in the Rockies: the wildflowers, jagged peaks, majestic canyons, gorges filled with tumbling meltwater, the brilliant stars in the velvet night sky, and the air so clear and sharp you can see a person from a mile away.

After that first spring in the mountains, none of us would ever again be ordinary men. Now, dressed only in the skins of animals we killed, we began the task of collecting our rich harvest of beaver furs. Then, having gathered all we could carry, we journeyed back east and sold them for a good profit.

CHAPTER 2

The following year, 1825, we set out again. Once more, we went through a cruel winter followed by a perfect spring. This was also the year of the first Mountain Man Rendezvous, an event that would be repeated for years to come. After surviving months of subzero temperatures, trapping beavers, and fending off wolves and grizzlies, all of us mountain men would get together. We'd swap tales, argue about the best and worst places to find furs, occasionally fight, and generally have a walloping good time.

The Rocky Mountains

This was the life I led for the next four years, trapping and exploring, meeting wild animals like eagles, grizzlies, mountain lions, elk, buffalo, deer, and beavers, and meeting even wilder men and having all kinds of treacherous adventures. There was the time my partners and I were making our way through the Snake River valley. We spotted smoke signals rising from the hills above us.

Soon after, we heard loud singing and saw about 500 mounted Indians galloping directly toward us. Horrified, we recognized them as Blackfeet, who were famous for their love of scalps!

We raced away, but as we did, an old man in our party took an arrow in his back and tumbled from his horse. I turned, hoping to rescue him, but six Blackfeet fell on him and scalped him before I could lift a finger.

We now reached a clump of willow trees where we saw a group of about thirty men, women, and children crouched in the bushes, screaming in utter terror at the sight of the approaching Indians.

CHAPTER 2

Realizing that we must not let the Blackfeet reach the women and children, about fifty of my companions and I turned our horses and charged back at the Blackfeet, firing as we did. Soon, Indians were crashing from their horses, brought down by our bullets and **musket balls**.

Clinging to my horse's mane like grim death, I bent low and rode through the Blackfeet lines, wounding some six or seven as I did. I now galloped back down the river valley, knowing about 200 trappers were camped a mile to the south.

CHAPTER 2

Half an hour later, I led those trappers in a furious attack on the Indians. After a ferocious battle that left dozens of them dead and the rest galloping off in a panic, we got through to the trapped women and children who, thankfully, were all unharmed.

Then there was the time when a group of my pals and I were sitting outside our tents, chatting in front of a huge log fire. All of a sudden, we heard a thunderous whooping noise, accompanied by a terrible roaring. We looked up to see a mob of Blackfeet charging into our camp.

At first, we could not understand where the earsplitting roaring was coming from. Then we saw that the Blackfeet were driving an enormous grizzly bear straight toward us!

For a few minutes, there was total chaos. The Indians ran off screaming with laughter at their brilliant joke and the great animal swayed furiously, swiping wildly with its huge claws. My companions all clambered up trees faster than frightened squirrels, and I was left cornered by the grizzly, with nothing but my knife to defend myself.

As the bear lunged at me, it let out a deafening roar. I thrust my hand into its mouth and seized its tongue. Then, with all the force I could summon, I used my other hand to plunge my knife into its chest.

A second later, a shot rang out and the bear crashed to the earth, a musket ball in its head. One of my companions had saved my life!

So as you can see, life was constantly full of surprises, and, not long after my brush with the grizzly, it took a new, and very unexpected turn indeed.

CHAPTER 3

Bull's Robe Beckwourth

I was at the Rendezvous and summer camp of 1828, when an old trapper told me how, just for a joke, he'd told the Crow Indians that I was really one of their own tribe. I'd been kidnapped from them by the Cheyenne years ago, then sold to the whites. He said that when he told them, the Crow became very excited and wanted me back. Well, the two of us had a good belly laugh and then thought no more of it. As it turned out, that wasn't the end of the matter – far from it.

The following winter, Jim Bridger and I were out setting traps, when we decided to split up. He took one fork in the river and I headed up the other. We hadn't been parted for long when I came across a herd of horses

CHAPTER 3

grazing at the riverside. Too late, I realized they were Indian mounts, but by now the two Crows guarding them had pounced on me. They were soon marching me into their village, where I was quickly surrounded by at least a thousand Indians. I was petrified. Then, to my relief, a whole swarm of Crow came rushing out of their tepee and began hugging and kissing me just like the long-lost relative they believed I was!

So began that period of my life when I lived as a Crow Indian. In no time, I was reunited with my long lost "sisters." Then, not long after that, I met the lovely Pine Leaf. Out of the eight Crow women I loved, there wasn't one to touch her. She was beautiful, brainy, and brave, and she could ride a horse and fight as well as any man.

When she was only twelve, her twin brother had been killed in a raid on our village. She had vowed that she would not marry until she had killed a hundred of the enemy with her own hands. Well, I did ask her to marry me. She said she would, but not

CHAPTER 3

until the pine leaves turned yellow. At first this pleased me, but then it occurred to me that pine leaves never do turn yellow, but stay green all year long. I knew I had been rebuffed and was immediately heartbroken.

Naturally, my life with the Crow wasn't all falling in love and getting married. Much of it involved hunting buffalo, stealing horses, and battling it out with our tribal enemies. Often, I would go out with raiding parties of young braves and attack the Blackfeet, Arapaho, Cheyenne, and Sioux, and, as a result of my heroism in these battles, I was soon made a chief. I was known among my Crow brothers as Enemy of the Horses and Bull's Robe.

One battle that particularly sticks in my mind concerns the time we were out hunting buffalo.

We were in a party of about 500, led by a chief named Long Haired Chief (on account of his hair, which measured some eight feet long). We'd been gone from camp about four days when we came across a large band of Blackfeet. They were well into our territory, but they had positioned themselves on a hilltop and were protected all around by huge rocks that made the place a natural fortress.

We sent for reinforcements, and 200 more of our braves arrived. Then all 700 of us descended on the Blackfeet, whooping and bellowing and firing on them with rifles and bows and arrows.

However, so well were they dug in that our charges were repeatedly driven back, with many of our braves sinking to their knees, pierced by arrows and felled by bullets. It soon began to look like we wouldn't be able to move the enemy.

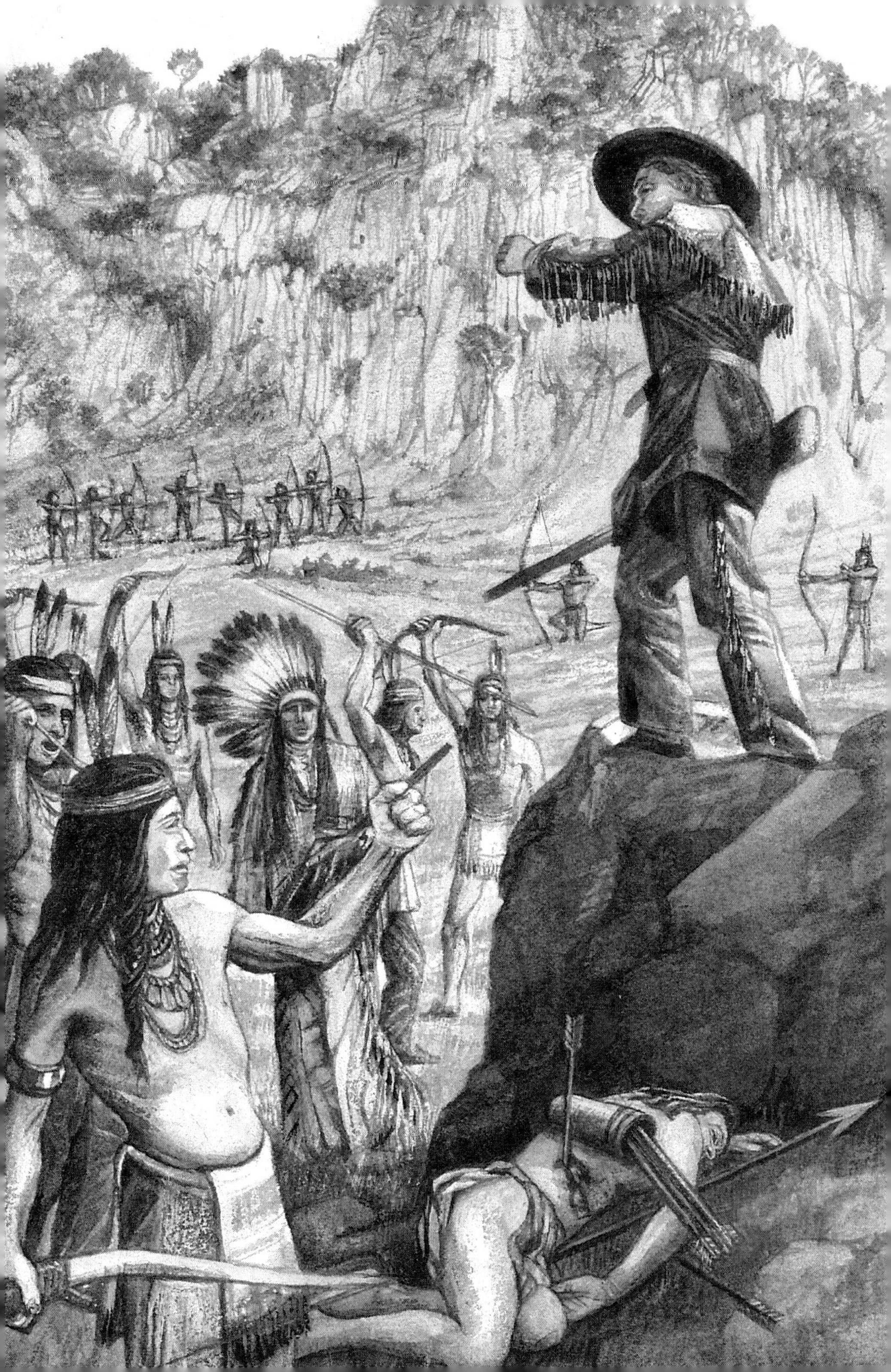

Many of our group, including Long Haired Chief, wanted to abandon our attack, but by now my blood was boiling. I leaped on to a rock and cried to the chief, "We can kill all of these Blackfeet, but if we run, we will be shot in the back. The Great Spirit has sent these enemies here for us to kill! If we don't, he'll drive away our buffalo and destroy our grasslands. No! We must fight. Follow me and I'll show you how the braves of the white chiefs fight!"

With that, not fearing for my safety, I sprung nimbly from the rock and sprinted toward the Blackfeet, looking neither to my right nor left. As I did, I heard a ferocious screaming and shouting from behind me, and I knew that the Crow were following, urged on by my mighty speech. Soon, we were scrambling up the rocks that surrounded the Blackfeet and engaging them in brutal hand-to-hand fighting.

I was instantly ambushed by two Blackfeet. One of them clung to my back, while the other jabbed at me with his hunting knife as

CHAPTER 3

I staggered this way and that to avoid his thrusts. Reaching up, I seized the one on my back and pulled him over my shoulders, held him above my head, whirled him around a few times, then flung him on top of his comrades. Then, before either of them could recover, I pulled out my pistol and blasted them both lifeless.

I now looked around me and saw that all over the hilltop my fellow Crow had gained the upper hand in our battle against the Blackfeet, and soon the enemy were surrendering by the hundreds.

Reader, I will not continue, for what happened next is just too awful to tell. However, in another twenty minutes or so, every single one of the Blackfeet lay dead.

After this battle, I was disturbed by the Crows' vicious behavior and decided that I would leave them. Yet, as it turned out, I had now become a hero, and whenever they were threatened by enemies, the Crow would come to me. This made it extremely difficult for me to leave.

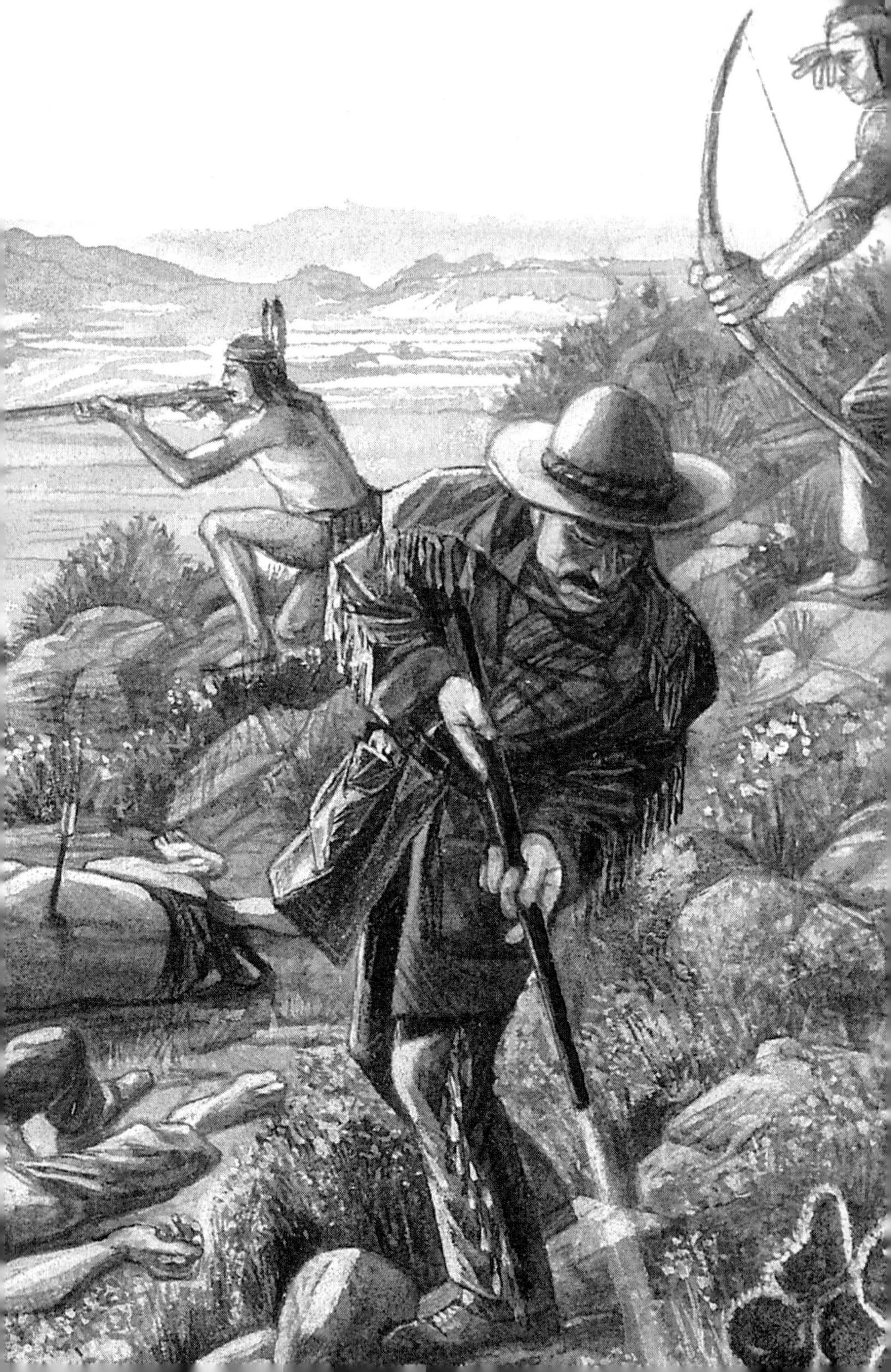

CHAPTER 3

Of course, it suited me in some ways, since I was now in a good position to conduct profitable trade with the Crow. They badly needed guns and ammunition, and the fur companies needed elk skins, beaver pelts, and buffalo robes. I was able to arrange these exchanges.

So I continued my life with the Crow, learning their language and all of their ways – and those of other tribes too. Then, after six years or so of me relentlessly asking her to be my bride, Pine Leaf finally said "yes," and we were married.

Five weeks after we were wed, I left the Crow for good and returned to St. Louis. You may say this was a strange thing to do, but I am a restless man, always in search of new horizons. I think that, maybe, it was the challenge of making Pine Leaf my wife that had kept me with the Crow for so long. Maybe not. In any case, I was definitely ripe for new adventures.

CHAPTER 4

Swamp Warfare

View of St. Louis in 1836

When I got back to St. Louis in 1836, I hardly recognized it. Only a few years before, when I had worked there with the blacksmith, it had been a cluster of shacks and muddy roads. Now it had paved streets, shops, warehouses, a theater, and magnificent mansions where rich people lived. Yet this was the way with so many cities in our fast-growing nation. They sprang up overnight!

As I walked around, I kept my eyes peeled for trouble. Friends had cautioned me that large sums of money had been offered for my life, as it was thought I had been involved when the Crow had robbed some white men.

After some time, I decided to visit the new theater, and during the intermission I went into the saloon for refreshments. As I did, five dangerous-looking characters advanced, looming over me. One of them said, "There's the Crow!" and they swiftly drew their knives. I, too, pulled my knife from my belt in readiness for a fight. I was in the middle of sounding a blood-curdling Crow war cry prior to hurling myself on my enemies, when the local sheriff walked into the bar. He ordered me to be quiet, and although I was seething with rage, I did as he said. Moments later, my attackers walked off. I tried to follow them, but the sheriff threatened to throw me in jail, so I left.

I now knew I had many enemies. This fact was confirmed when I heard a terrible rumor that was going around. It was being said that

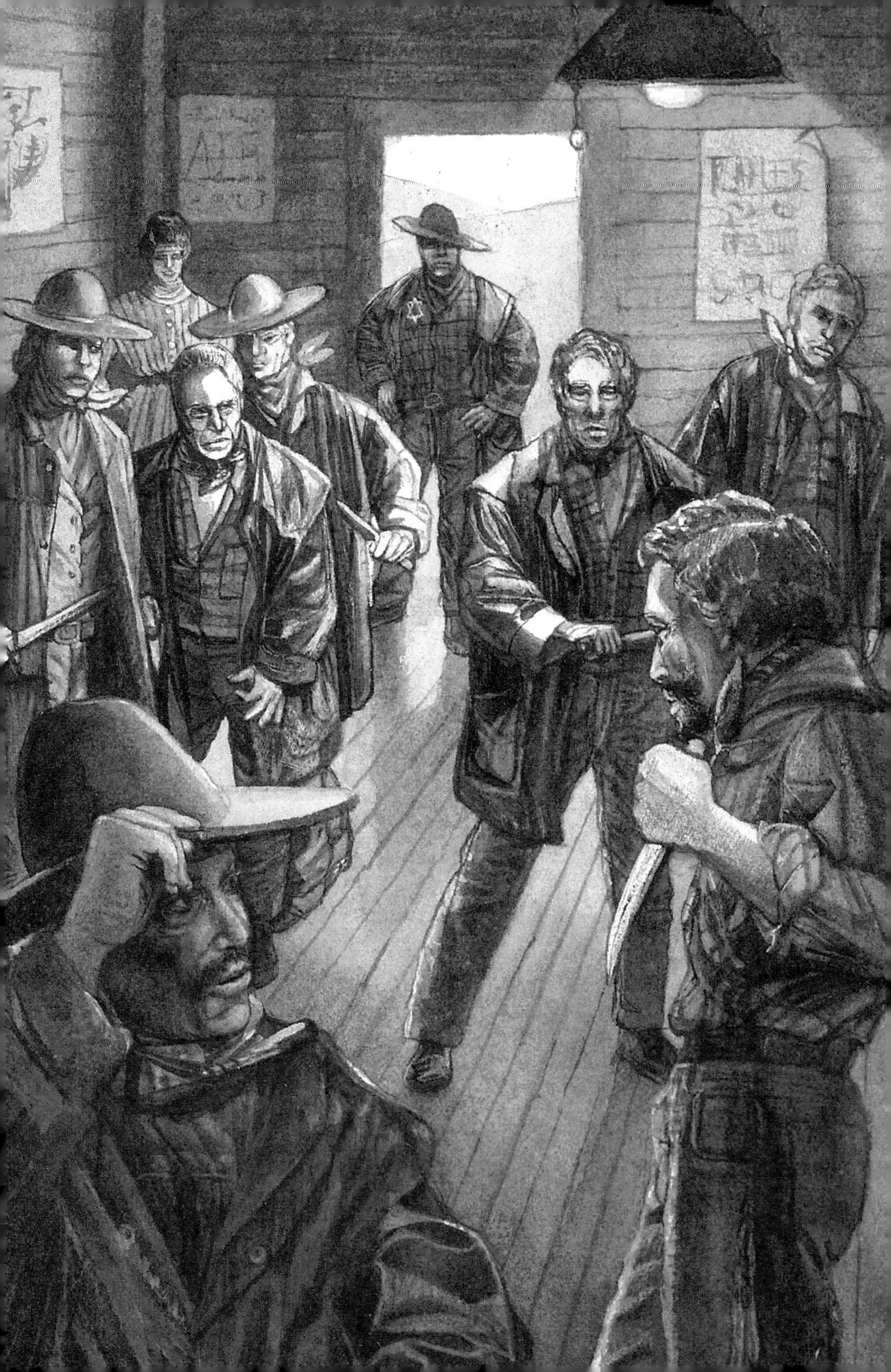

I was responsible for a plague of smallpox that was now sweeping through the Crow nation and killing many thousands of my old friends. This lie hurt me profoundly.

By the autumn of that same year, I was already tiring of town life and anxious to be off to the wilds again. The fur trade wasn't what it used to be, though. Jobs were few and far between. So when a friend told me scouts

CHAPTER 4

were being recruited for a campaign against the Seminole Indians down in the Florida Everglade swamps, I pricked up my ears, especially when I learned what a warm and pleasant place Florida was. Hoping to find fame and fortune, I traveled to New Orleans, where I joined up as a scout and express rider.

"Seminole" means "wild wanderer," and these Indians had fled to the swamps of Florida to escape the westward spread of the white settlers. They weren't the only fugitives in the Everglades. Black slaves who'd run away from the plantations also hid out in the swamps, and some of them married Seminoles. The planters wanted their slaves back, though, and the government wanted the swamps, so General Zachary Taylor organized a force of 800 men to drive out the Seminoles.

In New Orleans on October 26, 1837, we boarded small boats with our horses, but, not being accustomed to sea travel, we didn't secure them with ropes. This was a mistake we would soon regret. We hadn't been at sea long when terrible storms began to toss our boats like matchsticks, throwing the poor terrified horses every which way, killing some, and breaking others' legs.

To top off this tragedy, my boat became stuck on a reef. We were stranded for twelve days. Still more of our horses died of starvation and had to be thrown overboard.

CHAPTER 4

We finally made it to the steamy swamps, and on Christmas morning our camp was surrounded by a force of some 400 menacing Indians and black slaves. The Battle of Okeechobee began!

The enemy were shrewd. They hid up moss-covered trees and popped up all over the place. They fired their rifles, then dashed off through the swamps, leaving us all with our mouths gaping in amazement. Incredibly, they appeared to run across the surface of the water!

Of course, as we soon discovered, they hadn't run across the swamp at all. They had simply jumped from one underwater hummock to another. Not knowing where these hummocks were, we didn't dare follow. We feared we might drown or be attacked by the giant alligators and water snakes that lurked everywhere.

Eventually, the Indians and slaves slipped away into the woods, leaving over a hundred of our men killed or wounded. Despite the fact that only eleven Indians were killed, our leaders decided we had achieved a great triumph. I had to ride from one fort to another crying, "Victory!" at each – although I knew it was a bald-faced lie.

After the battle, I stayed on in Florida for another ten months, scouting and carrying messages. Soon, though, the monotony got to me, and I longed to be off horse thieving. The Seminoles had no horses worth stealing, so I decided once more to return to St. Louis and get myself a fresh job.

CHAPTER
5

Sante Fe to California

I'd only been in St. Louis for five days when I was hired by Louis Vasquez. He wanted to trade with the Indians of the southern plains. Another chance for excitement! I would be dealing with the Cheyenne, Arapaho, and Sioux, all enemies of my old tribe, the Crow.

We set out on the **Santa Fe Trail**, and, when we reached the trading post, Louis made me agent-in-charge. Now I had to find some Indians to trade with. I left the post, and after riding hard, I climbed a small mountain and spotted distant buffalo running in small groups. From this I deduced that they'd recently been chased by Indians, so I decided to stay put.

When darkness came, I saw campfires flickering, and I knew I had found the Cheyenne. In the morning, I went to them and said, "I have killed a great Crow chief and must run away or else be killed by his people. I have come to you, the bravest people on the plains, as I do not wish to be killed by any lesser tribe. I have come here to be cut up and thrown out for your dogs to eat."

Then I offered them gifts. Instead of killing me, they began to trade furs. I was in business! The friendship that I began with the Cheyenne that day would last for many years, until the terrible event that I'll recount later in the story.

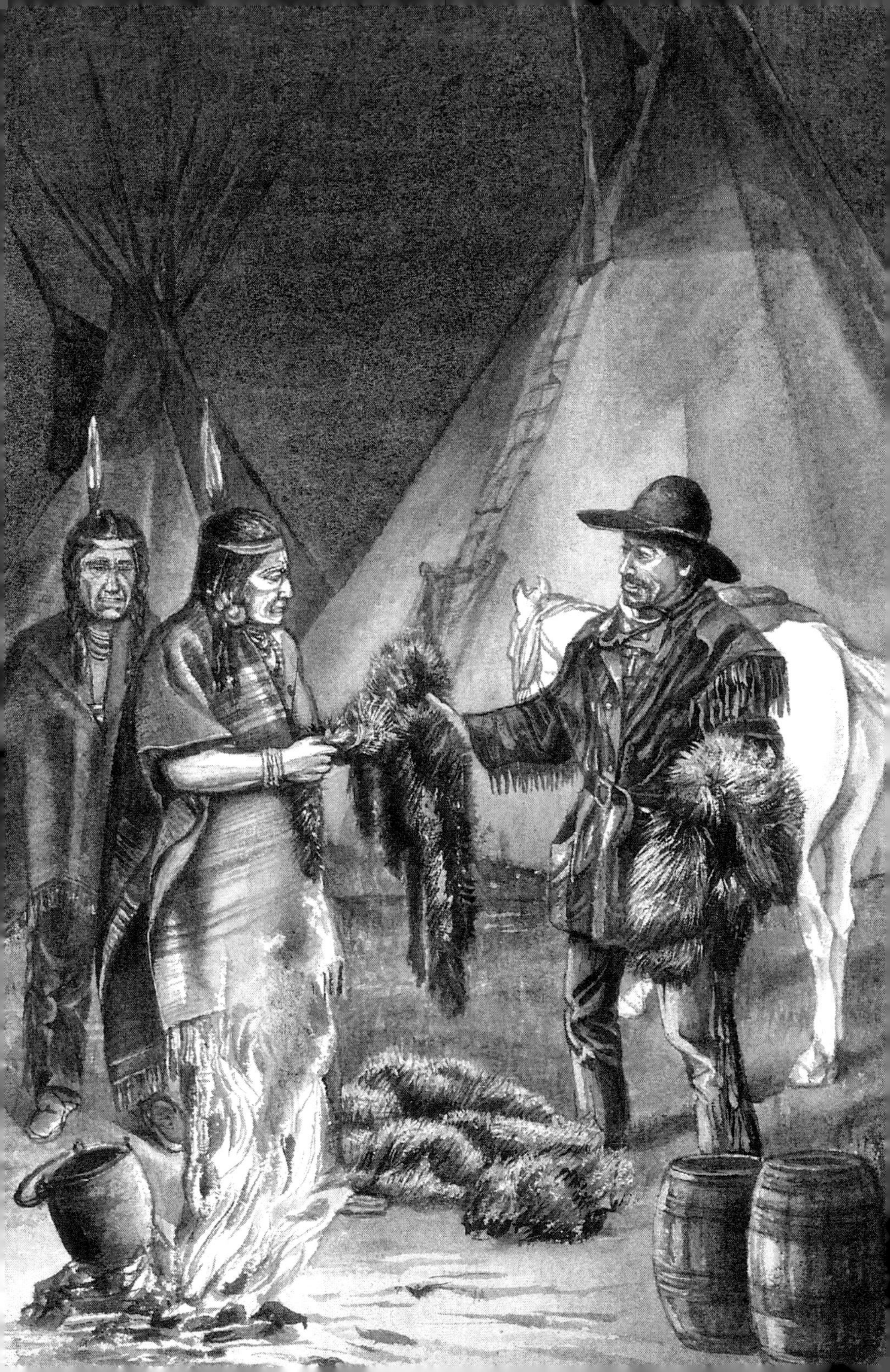

My stay at the trading post didn't last long, but during the next few years I continued trading and moving around the Southwest until I ended up in Mexico. It was while I was here in 1846 that war broke out between Mexico and America. My five companions and I were now in the wrong place at the wrong time. Still, we thought we would make the most of this situation, and we set to work stealing horses from Mexican ranches.

Very soon, we'd collected a respectable little herd of about 2,000 animals, which we then began to drive back to America. Of course, the Mexicans didn't take kindly to having their horses stolen, and they began to chase after us, firing their guns and yelling in an enraged frenzy.

It was a thrilling chase, which lasted about four days. As all these hundreds of horses thundered across the plains and splashed through rivers, we occasionally caught sight of our pursuers and saw puffs of rifle smoke, then felt their bullets go whistling past

CHAPTER 5

A band of horse thieves returning from a raid into Mexico

our ears. We had one advantage, though. Our pursuers were mounted on one horse each, but we had hundreds! Whenever our horse tired, we'd simply leap, midgallop, from its back to that of the nearest mustang. In this way, we eventually lost the Mexicans.

Back in America, I took a job carrying messages and acting as a guide and interpreter for the army. I also bought a hotel in Santa Fe, which my partner tended to while I carried out my army duties. The war continued for two more years, until America won and took over all of northern Mexico, which then included California.

I continued to work as an express rider, often crossing dangerous Indian territory, and during my journeys, I was frequently chased by belligerent tribes. On one occasion, I was trapped between two large war parties of Pawnee Indians. To add to my troubles, my horse was worn out, so I had no choice but to dig myself into the ground.

I huddled down in my hidey-hole like a scared jackrabbit and pulled some big rocks

CHAPTER 5

on top of myself. Minutes later, I listened to the Pawnees galloping this way and that as they searched intently for me. One of them almost rode his pony on top of my head! My heart thumping like a war drum, I stayed curled in my burrow until I was sure it was safe to come out. Then I stole a fresh horse and continued my journey.

In 1848, my feet became itchy, so I traveled to California where I became an express rider once again. It was while I was delivering the mail in this new job that I witnessed a most horrific tragedy, the hideous memory of which remains with me still.

On my various journeys delivering mail, I often rested at the Mission of St. Miguel. I liked this place because it was run by Mr. Reed, an Englishman, and he and his family were most enjoyable company. On this occasion, I arrived at dusk, and as usual I walked in, but was surprised that there was no one around.

I then went into the kitchen and saw someone on the floor fast asleep, or so I thought. I pushed the man with my foot, but he didn't wake up or move. It was then that I realized something had gone terribly awry.

I quickly went to my horse and got my pistols, then returned to the dark kitchen. Lighting a candle, I began to search the house. In the corridor, I stumbled over something slumped on the floor. I held my candle out, and with horror I saw that it was the body of a woman!

I now entered a room, and there I found yet another body, which I recognized as that of the Reed family's Indian maid.

CHAPTER 5

I was about to enter the next room, but as my hand reached for the doorknob, a warning voice in my head told me to stop.

Panic-stricken, I quickly left, found my horse, and galloped ninety miles to the nearest town for help. I returned to the mission some time later with a **posse**. On entering the house, we found no fewer than eleven murdered people!

The dead included Mr. Reed and his wife and children. Near to them, someone had tried to start a fire, obviously intending to burn the mission and them in it.

Some time after this, four wicked white men were arrested and found guilty of the murders. They had been guests of the Reeds, who had generously given them beds and food. Oh, and I had been right not to open that door. The murderers later confessed that they were on the other side of it, their pistols cocked, ready to do me in should I attempt to enter their hiding place.

As you might imagine, I decided to try my luck elsewhere.

The year before, a man named John Sutter had spotted a chunk of gold in his millstream, and thousands of people were now racing to California, hoping to strike it rich. Many had, too – some even by accident.

One man was sitting on a rock feeling homesick and dispirited because he hadn't found gold, so he got up and kicked the rock. The rock rolled aside and revealed an enormous gold nugget!

Pioneers mining for gold

CHAPTER 5

Prospector panning for gold in 1890

Another bunch of prospectors were burying their dead friend, and while the preacher droned on they began pushing at the dirt from the grave with the shovel. The next moment, one yelled, "Gold!" Yes, it was in the grave! The preacher abandoned the sermon and everyone started digging.

I figured it was time I got in on the act and looked at California's goldfields.

CHAPTER 6

My Beautiful Valley

Folks were striking it rich in the hills of California, but I didn't want to spend my days crouched over freezing streams panning for gold. Instead, I moved from one frontier town to the next, playing the card game they call monte.

I'm a pretty fair gambler, and some nights I won thousands of dollars. Still, money is of no great importance to me. I spent my winnings buying drinks for every man in town. Any I had left, I gave to the poor.

In 1850, I tired of gambling. I headed into a wild and lonely region of the Sierra Nevada mountains with some friends, and, while they panned for gold, I went off hunting.

It was while I was tracking a deer that I noticed a distant mountain pass that seemed significantly lower than all the others. I suspected that this might lead right through from the Sierra to California.

At this time in America's history, thousands of people from the East were trying to make their way west to a new life in California, which many saw as paradise on Earth. However, in order to make the move, they first had to cross the Sierra Nevada mountains. This was a most difficult journey, compounded by combative Indians, freezing blizzards, grizzlies, and wolves.

In 1846, a wagon train of about ninety people had become snowed in up in the Sierra Nevada mountains. Half had frozen to death, and the survivors were forced to eat not only their own pets, but also their dead companions! A new and quicker route through the Sierra would mean that wagon trains would be much safer. With this in mind, my companions and I decided to explore that distant pass.

After many days trekking across towering, snow-covered peaks, we entered an enormous grassy valley full of wildflowers and extraordinary birds. Flocks of ducks and geese sailed over our heads or swam on the crystal-clear waters of the river, which meandered along the valley. Not one of the creatures was the slightest bit afraid of us.

It was then that I knew that, save for a few Indians, no one had ever entered this breathtaking valley before. I also knew that it would make an ideal wagon route into California.

My friends and I now began making a road through the valley, and in July 1851,

CHAPTER 6

I proudly led my first wagon train of settlers over my pass to California. Soon, long lines of covered wagons were gradually climbing through the mountains and into that beautiful valley.

In 1852, I built myself a trading post in this lovely spot. Now the tired and hungry settlers would have somewhere to rest and stock up on supplies before the last leg of their journey into sunny California. My new home was in the most perfect place on Earth.

The scenery was awe-inspiring, the grass lush, the water plentiful, and the risk of attack by Indians slim. I soon had fields brimming with vegetables growing around my little homestead, flocks of contented sheep grazing the meadows, and a hundred or so fine ponies. I was constantly busy with the wagon trains that never failed to stop. I sold them food and supplies, repaired their **prairie schooners,** and gave them advice as well as the encouragement they so sorely needed.

Then, as has always been the case in my life, after seven years of being snug and happy in my beautiful valley, things changed. I'd been having a few problems. People had been failing to pay for my services, and there had been rumors flying around about me and stolen ponies. Also around this time, I organized a foot race between a black boy and an Indian boy. On a wild impulse, I bet everything I owned on the black boy to win.

Knowing the Indian boy was a good runner and not wanting to lose everything, I took the precaution of finding another black boy,

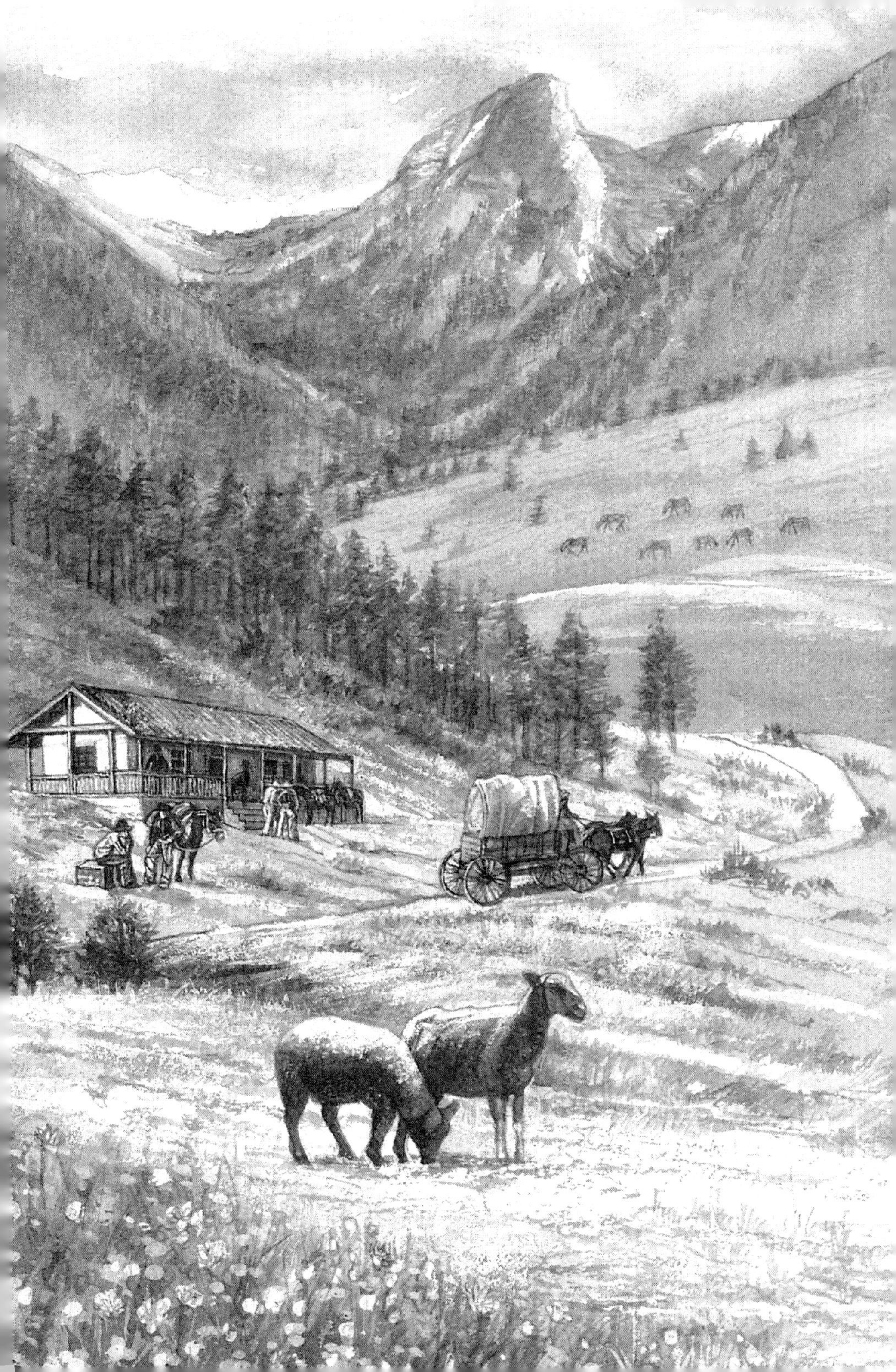

about the same size and appearance as the first. I had him hide behind a tree, about halfway around the one-mile race course. Then, when the first boy reached him, he slipped out from behind the tree and sped off on fresh legs.

Yet luck wasn't with me that day. Despite being rested, he still didn't catch up with the

CHAPTER 6

Indian boy, who ran like the wind. I wound up losing almost everything. Well, I shrugged off my bad fortune. Then, deciding that I was getting too old to endure another mountain winter anyway, I saddled up my remaining horse and journeyed back east, calling on old Indian friends as I traveled.

CHAPTER 7

My Betrayal of Friends

After many scrapes and adventures, I eventually landed in Denver, Colorado, where I opened up a store and saloon. Well, as has happened so often, trouble soon sought me out in my new life as a storekeeper and saloon owner.

One day, when I was laid up in bed with a fever, a ferocious giant of a man named Bill Payne came to my saloon looking for a fight. While talking to my barmaid, he suddenly tried to wrench her ring off her finger. Hearing her screams, I rushed downstairs and told Payne to leave, but he refused. Then we both saw a double-barreled shotgun in one corner of the room, grabbed it, and began to struggle.

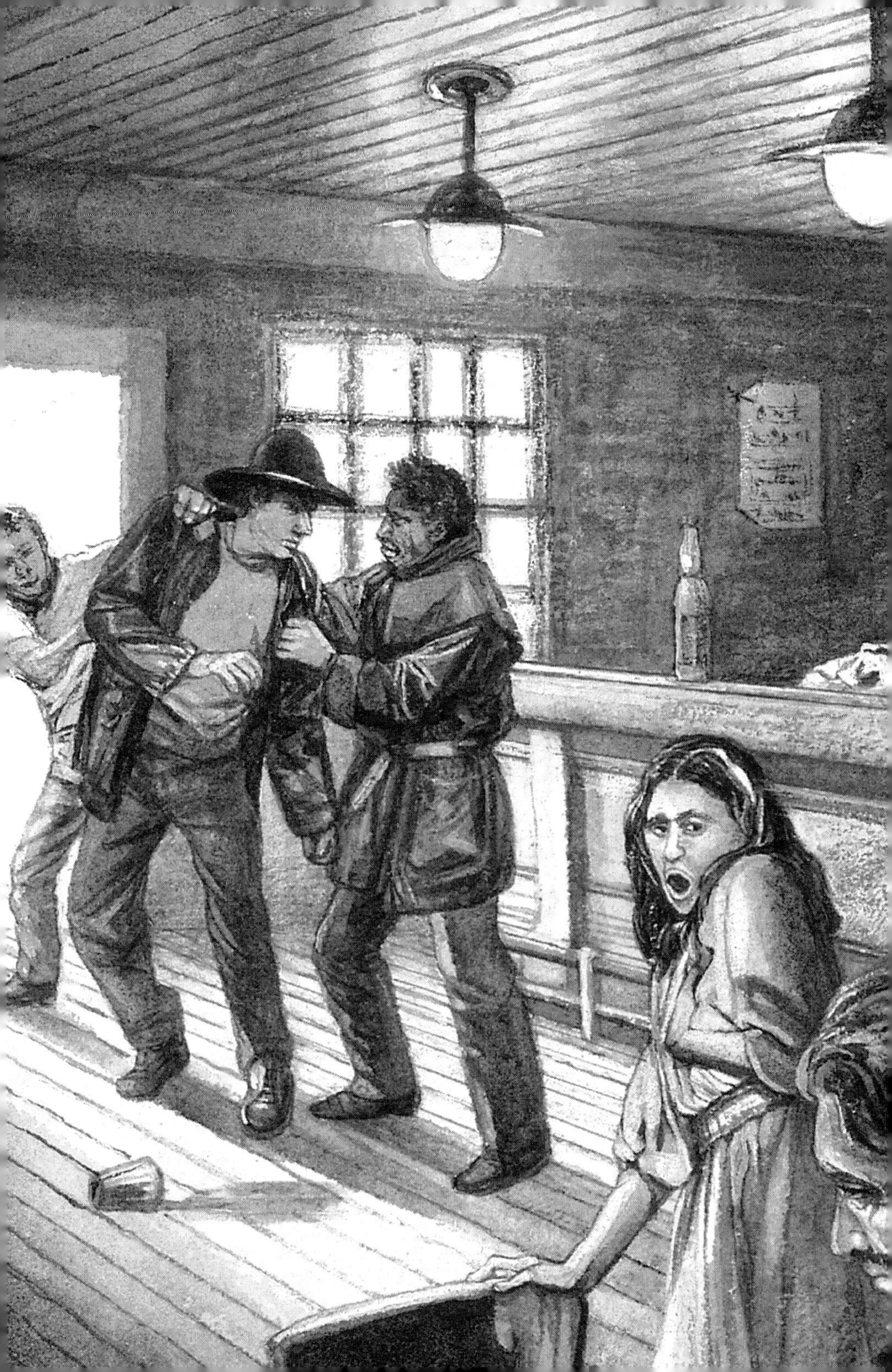

At this moment, two of my customers came to my rescue and helped me throw Payne out of the saloon. Payne was back in minutes, though, and, as he rushed at me, I seized the gun and shot him.

Roaring with pain and anger, he now crashed from room to room before falling into the fireplace and dying. Half an hour later, I was charged with Payne's murder and locked in the town jail. My trial followed soon after, and when it was time for the jury to give their verdict, every one of them said, "Not guilty!" Some even told me later I'd done a good job, getting rid of one of Denver's most notorious troublemakers.

Not long after my trial, the citizens of Denver were in a state of panic following Indian attacks on the outlying settlements. Colonel John Chivington decided that the way to solve the problem was to slaughter all the Indians in the area. He formed a special regiment of some 750 men to do just that.

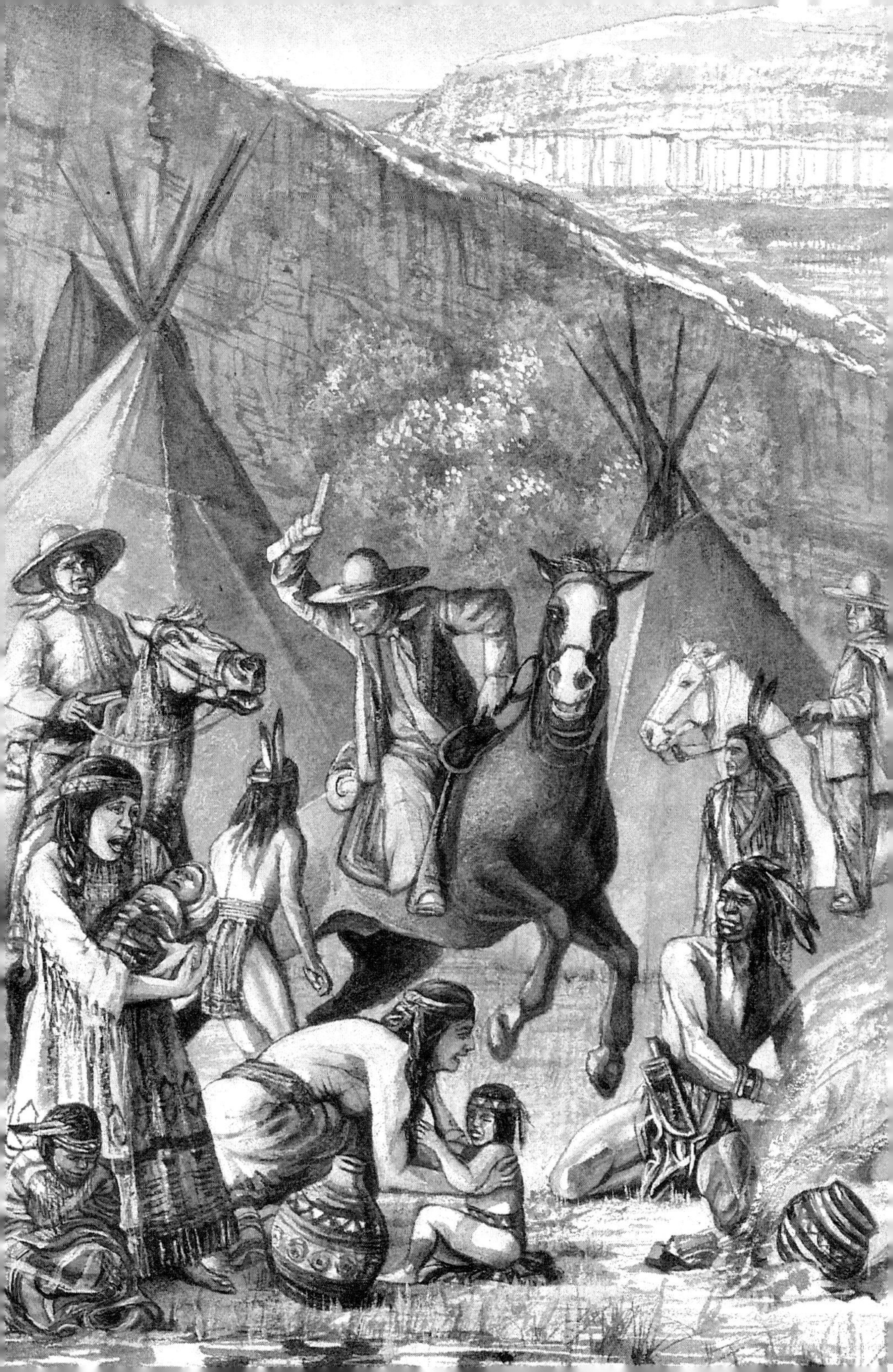

Because of my expert knowledge of the Cheyenne, I was approached to act as their guide. I didn't want to, as I knew the local Cheyenne were quiet, peaceful people, but Chivington was out for blood. Fearing he'd hang me if I refused, I did as he asked and led him and his men to Sand Creek, the place where I knew the Indians were.

When we finally reached the ridge overlooking the camp, we saw the tepees of Chief Black Kettle and his people spread along the riverbank below us. I knew that all those Indians were innocent and completely unprepared for an attack, believing they were protected by a peace treaty.

Colonel Chivington then gave orders to begin the killing, and his men charged down on the unsuspecting Cheyenne, shooting as they went. From my spot on the ridge I saw an old friend, Spotted Antelope, come running out of his tepee, shouting, "Stop! Stop!" but they shot him and six or seven children who were playing at the river's edge and a group of women standing by the cooking pots.

CHAPTER 7

During the next three hours, hundreds of innocent Indians, from one week to eighty years old, were killed by the whites, who only lost nine men. Afterward, the puffed-up soldiers paraded through the streets of Denver, trumpeting their victory, while crowds cheered them to the skies. To think I was part of that terrible day fills me with an unbearable shame that will stay with me forever.

After the brutal massacre, the Indians went on the warpath. Because of my terrible betrayal, my own conscience wouldn't let me alone, and early last year, I set out to find the camp of the Cheyenne.

After several days, I came upon their tepees and entered the lodge of Leg-in-the-Water. To my utter humiliation, he asked if I'd brought more white men to finish killing Indian families. So I told him I'd come to ask the Indians to make peace with the whites because there were now just too many for them to fight.

Then he told me the Indians didn't care if they died fighting the whites, because they'd taken and killed everything they loved: their prairies, forests, rivers, horses, buffalo... and now their families.

I understand what he meant. As the settlers move ever westward, I, too, am seeing the wild open spaces and wonders of nature I love so dearly disappearing as they build more and more towns and cities.

It's 1866 now, and I'm an old man. In my lifetime I've seen much of America change from wilderness to civilization, and I often try my best to envision what this remarkable country will look like 150 years from now.

CHAPTER 7

Will the great herds of buffalo still roam the prairies? Will bands of braves still gallop across the plains, yelling with the sheer joy of being alive in this magnificent country that the Great Spirit created?

All this talk of Indians has got me thinking of my old friends, the Crow, so I'll stop writing now and pay them a visit. It's been good putting all this down for you. I hope you've enjoyed reading it as much as I've enjoyed writing it.

James Pierson Beckwourth

Story Background

October 1866

Epilogue

Jim Beckwourth did go to see the Crow, and while he was with them, he died. There are various stories about how this happened. Some say he simply got a nosebleed, then passed away. Others say that he went hunting buffalo, his horse threw him, and he was trampled to death. Still others say the Crow poisoned him so his spirit would stay with them forever. However he died, though, spending his last hours among the Indians seemed a very fitting end to his life.

Some of the resources I used as research for this story were: On microfiche, published by Harper and Brothers (1856), *The Life and Adventures of James P. Beckwourth, as Told to Thomas D. Bonner* – various reprints have followed – and *Jim Beckwourth* by Elinor Wilson (1972), published by the University of Oklahoma Press.

There is also an official Beckwourth website at **www.beckwourth.org**. To find out about other African American pioneers, you can visit **teacher.scholastic.com/researchtools/articlearchives/honormlk/pioneers.htm**.

Index

alligators, 50
beavers, 17, 24, 25, 26, 41
buffalo, 4, 5, 17, 26, 35, 36, 38, 41, 52, 76, 77
California, 8, 56, 57, 60, 61, 62, 63, 64, 65
deer, 4, 14, 17, 26, 62
eagles, 17, 26
elk, 17, 21, 22, 26, 41
grizzly bears, 4, 10, 30
hotel, 56
mine, 13
moccasins, 8
mountain lions, 4, 17, 18, 26
prairies, 76, 77
rivers 18
Rocky Mountains, 7, 15, 22–23
Sierra Nevada, 62, 63
tepees, 22, 23, 33, 74, 75
wagon trains, 5, 8, 63, 65, 66
water snakes, 50
wolves, 25, 63

Glossary

Bonaparte, Napoleon – a French military leader who created an empire during the eighteenth and nineteenth centuries

express rider – a person who delivered mail and messages on horseback

musket ball – a small metal ball used as ammunition in a gun called a musket

Norman Conquest – William the Conquerer's military conquest of England in 1066

plantation – a large area where a single crop is grown. Early American plantations used slaves as workers.

posse – a group of people summoned by a sheriff for peacekeeping

prairie schooner – a covered wagon used by the nineteenth-century pioneers in crossing North America

Santa Fe Trail – a long route used for trade and travel between Independence, Missouri, and Santa Fe, New Mexico